THE NATIONAL POETRY SERIES

The National Poetry Series was established in 1978 to publish five collections of poetry annually through five participating publishers. The manuscripts are selected by five poets of national reputation. Publication is funded by the Copernicus Society of America, James A. Michener, Edward J. Piszek, the Lannan Foundation, and the Andrew W. Mellon Foundation.

1992 Competition

SHORTER POEMS, by Gerald Burns
    Selected by Robert Creeley. Dalkey Archive Press

MY ALEXANDRIA, by Mark Doty
    Selected by Philip Levine. University of Illinois Press

LOST BODY, by Terry Ehret
    Selected by Carolyn Kizer. Copper Canyon Press

DEBT, by Mark Levine
    Selected by Jorie Graham. William Morrow & Co.

WHAT WE DON'T KNOW ABOUT EACH OTHER,
    by Lawrence Raab
    Selected by Stephen Dunn. Viking Penguin

LOST BODY

TERRY
EHRET

COPPER CANYON PRESS

Eight of these poems were published by White Mountain Press in *Suspensions,* a collaborative collection. "Dora Maar" first appeared in *San Francisco Poetry,* "Lost Body" in *Mapping Codes,* vol. 8/9 of *Five Fingers Review.* "The Truth" was published in the *Gualala Arts Bulletin.* "Reading Montale" is from the premier edition of *Vivo.* "Woman Flapping In The Wind" and "In The Bones Of My Face" were originally published in *Paragraph,* vol. 3 and 5. "At The End Of The Season The Apples" appeared in the 1992 Statewide Anthology of California Poets In The Schools. "Monsters, His Monsters" appears in the anthology *Love's Shadow.*

Publication of this book is supported by a grant from the National Endowment for the Arts. Additional support to Copper Canyon Press has been provided by the Andrew W. Mellon Foundation, the Lila Wallace-Reader's Digest Fund, and the Washington State Arts Commission. Copper Canyon is in residence with Centrum at Fort Worden State Park.

The text on page 57 and the hieroglyphs on the cover and in the *Papyrus* section are from *Love Songs of the New Kingdom,* translated from the Ancient Egyptian by John L. Foster and illustrated with hieroglyphs drawn by John L. Foster. Copyright © 1974 by John L. Foster. By permission of the translator and the University of Texas Press.

Library of Congress Cataloging-in-Publication Data

Ehret, Terry.
  Lost body : poems / by Terry Ehret.
       p.   cm. – (The National poetry series)
  ISBN 1-55659-057-1 : $11.00
  I. Title   II. Series
PS355.H66L67   1993
811'.54 – dc20   93-801

COPPER CANYON PRESS
Post Office Box 271, Port Townsend, Washington 98368

TABLE OF CONTENTS

What The Heart Repeats

7 / Anglo-Saxon Love Calls

8 / Monsters, His Monsters

9 / Hunger

11 / Reading Montale

13 / Lost Body

14 / How We Go on Living

A Woman Steps Out Of The Sky

17 / Fuchsia

18 / At Night It Belongs to Woman Like These

21 / Total Lunar Eclipse, August 14, 1989

23 / March Rains

27 / Raven

29 / A Second Look at Penelope

30 / Dora Maar

31 / Woman Flapping in The Wind

Native Language

35 / Night Prayers

38 / The Author of This Poem Will Grant an Interview

41 / In The Bones of My Face

42 / Yesterday, My Pockets Full

43 / Today I Didn't

44 / In The Desert a Fool Smiles

46 / The Truth

47 / Opening Session at the Poetry Conference

49 / At the End of the Season the Apples

Narrations Leading to the Number Nine

53 /

Papyrus: A Temporary Journey

60 / A man floats

61 / These legs are running

62 / Bang

63 / A lake. A night without a moon

64 / The eye begins to open

65 / Where is the woman

66 / Here is a ridiculous bird

67 / Memories: a coffin

68 / She does not know

69 / He curls up under the weight

70 / She says, he says

71 / A snake is easier

72 / Sometimes their legs

73 / There are waterfalls

74 / Ribbon blades

75 / Her beads will break

76 / The ghost of a child

77 / This cold river

WHAT THE HEART

REPEATS

Anglo Saxon Love Calls

What is it I wait for   at the boundary of sleep?
A strange world with two names: sea-drinking
sea-diving.   A bridge into darkness
spread out beneath the sun,   beneath the wine-berried madrone
Here on the edge of the known world   I hear taut sails tugging
like white knives,   the drum beating,
the fine grass folding,   gulls circling the wind.
They drop fast to the ground,   laughing in the long spring grasses.
Give me a brown-beard,   a beam-tingled sailor
to linger in my stream,   to loose this hardness in me,
sip the last of my heart's sweet.   Drink my wrath,
my golden, sunny boredom,   stroke under my skin,
circle me with gold,   glide down me like a river,
your tongue writing this dream,   this fine wire of my pleasure.
We were born here,   and here most likely we will die.
But for now the world is enough: the broad sea coast,
your fingers stroking my forehead,   sails darting across the wind.
Give me your unborn,   your broken promises.
We will hang them like ornaments   in the air,
our hearts strange and light,   our arms empty.
Press your foot on my foot,   my friend,
sweet taste of guessing,   drinking and swallowing,
our tongues circling,   calling and answering.
We sing out like peacocks   arching high.
Listen to the belly-song,   the wolf-yapping,
the fast-panting calypso.   This cold feels sweet and hot
tonight.   Now that we are no longer ourselves,
but two animals,   two smiling beasts.

Monsters, His Monsters

She went on swallowing monsters, his monsters
because he couldn't tell her that he didn't,
and because he couldn't tell her that
she waited. For his phone calls. For his letter.

Because he couldn't tell her that he didn't
(from the bottom of the stairs he couldn't)
she waited for his phone calls, for his letter.
Because he didn't, he couldn't tell her not to,

from the bottom of the stairs he couldn't.
She told him about the red blood and the hemorrhaging.
Because he didn't, he couldn't tell her not to.
She was swallowing monsters, she said,

she told him about the red blood and the hemorrhaging.
He could stand halfway down the stairs and look up at her.
She was swallowing monsters, she said.
He could watch the space between his feet.

He could stand halfway down the stairs and look up at her;
he couldn't tell her that he didn't want to;
he could watch the space between his feet;
he could leave. He would close the door behind him.

He couldn't tell her that. He didn't want to.
She went to live in his home town.
He could leave. He would close the door behind him.
She went on swallowing monsters, his monsters.

Hunger

She remembers a novel and the heroine who was dreaming of a baby. For seven nights it came to her, a scraping, withery cry. This was an omen: someone would die. The heroine would have to go away.

The flannel gown has two long slits that run down the middle of what look like folds in the material. She can pull the slits open and nurse the baby without having to undress. This makes it slightly less inconvenient. She thinks, there are three hours between feedings. In the novel the heroine's lover wanted to take her to live on the moon—a cave in one of the white valleys among the volcano tops. She would live with him there, and only him. She wonders, why didn't the heroine say something? She would starve, it was obvious, alone with him forever.

When she's angry her mouth resembles a square and she is all gums and fist. The breasts respond. There is no question of choice. Above the nipple a tightening and pressure of muscles contracting involuntarily. She holds the tiny, furious head in one hand and works the nipple into the baby's mouth until she latches on and begins to suck. Already milk has soaked the left side of the gown, and she knows before going back to sleep she will need to wash her breasts and change.

He wanted her. She was his, he said. Everything she felt, he felt, but the heroine was dreaming of a baby. She could see her lover on the road below like a speck on a white track. When she woke a single candle burned in the dark before her. A face leaped from the glass, a voice in the drapery. In the morning she did not recognize herself.

She remembers late nights before the baby. She liked it then because of the quiet and the feeling of being someone else and the only one awake. Maybe the sound of a truck on a hill on the other side of the city. Once the heroine woke up with the moon spreading across the ceiling. She began to talk to it as if she were standing in front of a window listening for a voice beside her saying, "You don't want to live in a German garden wearing ribbons. If you were a storm you would never touch ground."

He wanted to hold her. He wanted his lips on her lips. She works her index finger between the baby's gum and the nipple to break the suction. It is time for the other breast. She moves the safety pin to remind her which one to begin with next time, but it is more trouble than remembering. If she leaves the flap down, the air might help heal the painful hairline cracks. She touches the tip of the red nipple, molded by the baby's sucking, an alien landscape where small beads of blue-white milk pool in the crevices.

The heroine's lover came twice to her door during the night. She must have heard the knock, but was already watching the moon cross the ceiling. Would she have starved, alone with him? She was his, he said. The pride of his life and the desire of his eyes. The sharp thirst comes to her as it always does, so she reaches for the glass of water on the table beside the bed. She must have heard the knock, though. She must have known he would come. Even a child could understand hunger. Sometimes she felt it clinging to her neck and she had nothing at all to give it.

Reading Montale

When I come to the corner it is
Florence I smell

diesel fumes and bread baking.
I begin to sway as mothers do

a little back and forth.
But she is home and I

have come away on purpose not to hear
her—not to be called back again

from the river moving under
the triple arches of the old bridge. Still

she comes to me, my phantom child
pulling me

out of my sleep
slowly, the sky turning to blue

again. In a niche above the street
a woman with her baby framed

by dark green shutters
behind the coolness

of a room darkened in the afternoon
for rest. I have come to the window

hearing a baby cry.
My breasts are tight, the milk

comes of its own. I press
the palm of my hand against the nipples

to keep back the flow.
The river moves along the wall

as I remember it.
I stood on the scales and paid

fifty lire for my fortune
printed on a small white square:

date e ricevete di piu. I do not know
which is giving and receiving, how we say

what we need or want,
if it is easier to return

to the street where I am standing or to stay
at this window watching

the river bend back the night
to Florence.

Lost Body

AFTER "ANATOMY OF LOVE"
BY ULALUME GONZALES DE LEON

One less
           possible day
opening and closing. There
we awaken, about to cross over
into the province of our beloved name.
As if the danger of brandishing this body
belonged to another. We do not know
where our blood is taken,
why our eyelids throb,
whether our hands can translate
what the heart repeats, its remote
cry.
      One less possible day repeating
with our arms, our skin, our knees
and the amorous nape of the neck
what it is like to be a body.
To lie in wait, opening and closing,
crossing from this body into the only other possible.
We utter our forgotten name to one beloved,
as if to travel into that dangerous heart
were possible. As if it were possible
to be a body. As if we had never forgotten.

How We Go on Living

Salt on your window, on the wind together, always
and always in separate rooms,
splinters of broken glass;
we rest our hands on the table.
Only our breathing keeps us on the course we had charted.

The past comes easily to you. It also
reminds you of me:
all afternoon on the mattress
we sang useless madrigals

        tra-la   *li*

          tra   *la-la*

            tra-la-la   *la*

                     into our old age

        out of control, spinning.

We played hard and long into the night
fiercely, like Bengal tigers.
It was a celebration, a holiday.

But we singed our wings on the game, fell like
blossoms into our hands. I called your name
out loud: your heart I never questioned.

A WOMAN STEPS

OUT OF THE SKY

Fuchsia

When the center opens, spindly pistils, ballerina legs.

The resting point of a hummingbird, invisible to me
in the clutter of about-to-fly leaves.

Above the tree, high over the yard a flutter of white curtain
and the voice of a woman, the voice of a man
rising like leaves.

White moths whirl and tumble.
Even as they speak the spinning white arms
of a hurricane, the white
necklace of her islands, her salt wind, her windflowers.

We are always halfway from the other side,
halfway from our dark sister, spinning
far out on the edge of her white arms.

The light rising out of us, passing like years
into the dark history of space

again and again. The unfolding.

At Night It Belongs to Women Like These

"Fräulein"
>A car rolls up at the curb.

"Fräulein"
>The car speeds away.

"Excuse me, Fräulein, do you have a light?"
>Then the hand posed, cigarette before her.

"You're American?"
>>"Yes. Is it so obvious?"

"The blue jeans."
>>"Oh."

"My apartment is down the street, shall we go?"
>>"What?"
>>>"To my apartment."

"What do you mean?"

>Along the bridge the lampposts crouch,
>casting pools of yellow light
>the women move in and out of slowly,
>smiling.

"Well, you see you were walking here alone."
"It's so cool here in the street."
"Fräulein, there is always the Volkspark. This is the Maria Hilferstrasse. I must walk you to your hotel, then. Cigarette?"

2

It is best to be awake when others are sleeping. Late or early it is best to be very quiet and alone. Then you will call upon a spirit, something moving carefully and in inches, feeling close to the ground the heat, moving as you move quiet in the dark that is full of blood and breath. You will call upon a spirit to be with you. You will find a voice to speak to it. You will give it a name. It will speak to you.

Hu! Listen

In alahi yi
Elahiyi
Ayasta

Take them!
Unwind the jewels, the blue flowers.
Drink them!

Let your soul come to rest at the edge of your body.

Let the night begin in your hair.

Uhuwe-uhuwe
A ye-he
Ayasta

The breath of your mouth
is a flame blown loose,
the winds ride between your feet,
a moon,
a mist of silver foxes,
yellow-fire, fire-white

Ayasta
Elahiyi

The earth is rich with the lives of our skin.

3

A woman in the dark becomes full of night. Her mouth opens to the moon. She moves in and out of pools of light, smiling. She becomes complicated. And now that she is no longer laughing, she wishes to sing, she wishes to smoke. She wishes to take control of her breath, moving in and out, smiling.

In the cool of the night it grows full of women, full of hot rooms, and now how she loves the sound of her high heels clicking against the pavement. She loves to watch the windows rolling up and down, the cars speeding away. Then the hand posed, cigarette before her.

"Yes, is it so obvious?"
"The blue jeans."
"Oh."

At night she grows full of desire to be awake and to walk out into the street, it's so cool here in the street. She rises out of the bed and comes to the window. She wants to be out in the street alone and walking quietly.

She travels secretly, in and out.

Along the bridge the lampposts crouch, casting pools the women move in and out of slowly, smiling.

Total Lunar Eclipse, August 14, 1989

AFTER FRAGMENTS BY SAPPHO

Come, lean near
the white flame.

We will tell a story
to bring her back.

A story of her lover,
his longing, her bright arms.

A goatherd from the woods
beyond the temple

who wanders over the hills
under a cloak of stars

gathering hyacinths underfoot.
He sings, crushing the purple hyacinths,

calling out to her in the secret
names he gives her:

> *My long-fingered goddess,*
> *my forgotten one,*

> *come back,*
> *come roam these hills again with me.*

> *Come stain your feet with the juice*
> *from the young hyacinths.*

Come breathe deep the honey clover,
    the sweet elysium.

There is no pleasure like the delicate chervil,
    the gentle clover underfoot.

Hearing this she
lifts her blue veil,

her shadow-face.
Now the sea is brimming with light.

The bells at her waist ring
as she dances.

March Rains

Close to the west a great ocean is singing.
The waves roll toward me, covered with many clouds.
Even here I catch the sound.
I hear the rumbling.

RAIN SONG OF THE PAPAGO

Out where the dark sea swells,
the older men
want her. Their eyes
watch and smile obediently,
drinking the smell of her
small girl-breasts.

One approaches the window.
Beneath the ringing sun
a green ocean
pulls them
under its curve.

He places his lips on hers,
twin currents,
these blind channels,
and the sun beating down,
their backs rising, arching.

*   *   *

In the night the rain came.
It filled the gutters,
overflowed around driveways,
spurting up the holes of sewer covers
like a fountain, brown and terrible.
It formed around the pink stucco walls

of the elementary school
a broad, shallow lake
so that four hundred children filed
over a single board plank.
The gutters rose and became streams,
the streets long sheet of rain
pouring out of the hills,
and on the knoll of oak
at the top of the rise
where the road stopped and circled itself,
lake after lake,
arcing
into wet, bright air.

*   *   *

A woman steps out of the sky.
She steps out into her kitchen
in the morning light, presses
her face against the glass.
She is the woman of the stories,
the woman of the mist
whose hair men are afraid to smell,
afraid they will die,
lost
in the mist of her voice,
her singing, her rhythms.
From the kitchen the woman waits for her thoughts
to return, waits
for a way to connect this day
to any other, some pattern
in the coming and going.

She calls to her seeds,
her little ones.

*   *   *

Step over the low blue wall.
Step behind this quiet
translucence,
breathe, close your eyes, turn your back.

Remember what you were dreaming,
where you were traveling
before this water came to you.
Remember you are in a body now.
And the shape of it, covering you,
being you, over and over.

*   *   *

There are two skies.
One above us, dark winter night.
This is the sky I am traveling.
The one with the voice,
the one I fall into
if I lie still on my back on the dock.
Small boats bump and creak in the dark.
The other sky descends below us,
and floating in this sky,
this black and liquid one,
the same stars swinging the other way.

One beside me asks,
which direction are we going?
Are we rising or falling or circling back?

*   *   *

The day broke with slender rain.
I crawled into the mouth
under the green gravity of waves.

In the fine mist of the morning
I lay
quiet,
a saturated woman.

Young boys
playing in a field
of owl's clover,
star anise,
wet from the rains,

young boys found their way to me,
looking for a place to be dangerous,
to be so many men,
so many journeys,

long of leg, naked
rain boys.

They came for me,
wet from the fields,
wading through blue hyacinths,
young boys,
long of leg,
leaning into the grass.

Raven

Her wings are human hands
sprung from her shoulders and feet,

and her heart,
a dark eye.

In her there is no place of rest,
only fear retracting,

pulling away from the small
egg of earth.

She rises out of the dark
eye, wings extended.

This is the danger:
coming too close

you will cease
to exist. Awaken to

find yourself lodged
inside the other, wings

pressed tight against
your body.

This is the danger: flying too far,
burning wings,

the dark
center of your heart.

Voiceless,
she will come to you in the night.

She will come to your bed;
she will press a knife to your heart.

In the east, thunder
shakes down the white

blossoms of the apple trees.
You are in the eye,

the still center. She
presses her knife, calls to you

without a voice. Your dark
eye opens. She enters.

A Second Look at Penelope

Penelope waited a long time for Ulysses to return. She waited longer than most marriages last. Ten years of fighting and then probably only occasional news. Ten years more he wandered and then no news at all. But it seems she was good at long-distance relationships. Her patience, her long, long sadness gave her strength. One day her name would come to mean patience itself. What made it difficult were the nights, the ones in winter that begin early and grow colder every hour. Those nights her fingers turned numb, her knuckles ached. Pulling out strand by strand. A power. She kept undoing time, unlocking time. At night, alone in her bedroom, she would take down the lamp, hold it over her tapestries and one by one pull out the threads, ticking off the seconds, minutes, hours, backwards winding under and over, back through the lost years of wandering, through the tortuous beacon trails of war messages across the islands and mountains from the shallow bay below Troy, back further to the hot days in August she spent pushing her boy out into the world and feeling the pull of ocean in her groin. Back again past her bridal year, the marriage bed of olive-wood, the prayers and offerings of almond flowers in spring, back to her own girlhood, under and over the years unweaving white, red, gold, green, till time itself became no bigger than the edge of the waning moon in winter. She could see it out the window of her bed-room in the raw hours before dawn. In the first light, her hands stiff with the task of turning back time, she puts out the lamp, follows the thin tail of smoke curling toward the hall where the women of the court are already arriving, bringing flax and spindles, dyes and fingers quick to set the pattern right again, weaving the strands back together, working late into the afternoon. All day over and under, combing and smoothing the long hair of memory.

Dora Maar

He can wholly possess it only as long as she fits into
the picture that his imagination is always arranging.

FROM *Pablo Picasso* BY JAIME SABARTES

I hold my hand in my hand
below the frame
things are in place—so, just so.

Here is the dress I have always worn. Here is my hair, my mouth,
my jaw, my arms like two schoolgirls
awkward and fixed against my side
as if they ought not to be there at all
having no business being there at all.

"This part of the painting will be black," he says,
bending my elbow to fit a little
more into the lower edge. "It will be
dark, even monstrous, and you will not like it there.
On your forehead a furrow above the eyebrow
because when you look, there is an absence you want to fill
and it makes you very proud, very vulnerable—nothing dangerous.

"The death of your father sits behind you
on the wall that is gray. It moves
up from the floor in the lines of your dress,
over your breasts. But see, I will paint here a white collar
for you, white with a lace edge, because if I
were to take it away now not even a
red hat would keep you from breaking into
angles, your teeth clenched in your hand,
your eyes the eyes
of birds of prey."

Woman Flapping in the Wind

She wanted to sit at the window. She wanted the wind to blow in her black hair she had let down. She was an old woman with long black hair and she wanted to ride in the wind in the afternoon. She was an old woman with a daughter, an old woman with a son. She wanted the wind to blow in her black hair in the afternoon, and she pulled up the shade at the window. It made a wild flapping noise like a bat let loose in the bus. Her daughter told her to sit still. Her daughter pulled down the shade and closed the window. Her son moved to the back of the bus and looked away. She was an old woman. It was a hot afternoon and she an old woman in black. She wanted the window, she wanted to ride in the wind in her hair she had let down. Her daughter told her to sit still. She wanted the window open, she pulled up the shade. It made a flapping noise in the wind in her hair, her wild black hair she had let down. An old woman with a daughter who moved to the back of the bus with the son who was looking away. Together they held her. Together they held her still and someone at the front of the bus pulled down the shade and closed the window. Together they kept her still in their arms, her hair flapping in the wind. She wanted the wind. She wanted the window open. It was a hot afternoon and she started flapping wildly like a bat let loose in the bus. Together they held her. She was an old woman, she yelled, her arms making a wild flapping noise like a bat and she an old woman she yelled. She an old woman with long black hair flapping like a bat in the wind in the afternoon. She wanted the wind. She wanted to ride in the wind, her voice yelling and flapping in the wind.

NATIVE

LANGUAGE

Night Prayers

Invite the dark one in.

Give voice to the unseen, disquieting
world.

A heart beats in the darkness.
A telephone rings.
A voice—no longer my own—
no longer interested,
asks to be left undisturbed.

If chaos were only chaos, I might in time
sleep beneath the spring grasses.

When we arrive
beyond the word for everything,
each gesture
becomes a ritual.

Words stretch out of reach,

stones magnified in the bottom of a pool.

We rouse ourselves
to the effort of speech,
but we are already beyond it,
beyond time

out in the dark water
pressing against the lighted window
where we sit

lost in the orange petals
arranged on a plate before us.

Notes from the piano
rise toward me,
unfolding
sound,
stitching
this current of time
we move through.

World without nouns, without grammar.

If only the world were the known world.

Unfixed, the moon
sets
twice.

I walk home alone. Asphalt
glitters haloes
in the streetlight.
My feet ring metallic,
each step a note

ringing, my skin, my breath,

my memory of the way home
consumed in that ringing,
those unreal haloes.

Day and night
the lovely
abandoned things of the city
cry out for redemption:

Remember the apple trees in the yard next door;
remember the window frame, the light;
hold these long enough
to shape enough world to wake up to,
rise into, respond to.

This constant returning
to the body.

If only the world were the known world.
If chaos were only chaos.

Rising, falling
making and unmaking,

dark forms against
the light.

The Author of This Poem Will
Grant an Interview

Where were you when you wrote your first poem?

The one I consider the first, or the first?

The first.

I was in a bedroom on the Mendocino coast.

When was this?

August, 1968.

Were you alone?

No, the bedroom belonged to a small boy who would wake up
in the night and bang his head on the floor.
A thumping came through the dark
waking me up after a brief visit into a dream
which took an odd turn to include a door
so that the thumping would have some place to be coming from.
It continued longer than anyone might expect
unaccompanied by tears
or cries of pain. It must be that way
in hell, I think, where the damned
must keep punishing themselves to stop the pain.
And it must be
some part of us still remembering hell
that explains the skin torn off the fingers
or nails bitten to stubs,

the secret places on our body we uncover
to pinch or burn or pick at
as if idle hands
could be possessed by the souls in hell,
souls who watch us from the bottom of our drains
and know what we look like on the underside, know
what we have eaten for six thousand years,
that we tell lies in order to appear solid,
that really we have nothing whatsoever
in common with the living.

How old were you?

Twelve.

Why were you writing?

It gave purpose to my wanting to be alone,
to my walking away from the river
even though I wanted to be in the river where I was swimming
nude
On a Sunday, the first Sunday I had not gone to church
or been with my parents. The first time
I enjoyed doing a thing I would not tell in confession
which meant that next Sunday I would swallow him
and he would have to twist in pain inside me with that sin,
swimming in my girl-body, nude
in the sun
along the Navarro
in front of men who had penises I could see.

Did you write to do penance? To disappear, so to speak, through the upper right-hand corner of things?

No.

I went to sleep and the thumping continued.

In the Bones of My Face

In the bones of my face, the long bones of my face, the bones of my long face, my long face my long long face, my clear long willow my wan, my whisker, my water, my wing, light, wing my light, leaf light, leaf, leaf, leaf leaf round, leaf round round, leaf round in the crease, in the wet crease, in the wet wide crease in the ease, in the ease, in the slow, slow, ease, in the slow, in the slow slow old, in the old of my aunt, my old Aunt Eda, Aunt Eda, my old old aunt, my Eda.

Yesterday, My Pockets Full

AFTER GHAZAL IV BY GHALIB

I arrived yesterday, my pockets full of candles lit after
        the guests were gone.
While they were here we kept the lights on since there
        was nothing to be gained.

An infinity of selves: reflections of a folding mirror.
All the heads turn to look at the same time.

There is an impulse to shut the door on the landscape
and concentrate instead on arranging the furniture.

Everything gets erased by this profound interest in farming.
One would know then how much the ground could be trusted.

I have never carried razors in my mouth on purpose.
You'll have to believe this unless you wish to believe
        something else.

Today I Didn't

Today I didn't ring a quiet bell. I didn't turn my head and eyes to look in all directions. I didn't remain alert for at least one hour at a time. I didn't have sustained interest in details. Today I didn't write a letter. I didn't lift my leg. I didn't sing a lullaby. I didn't swat a fly. I didn't remove the dead bee from between the screen and the window. Today I didn't open the window. I didn't brush my hair. I didn't flick ashes from a cigarette. I didn't move when the baby cried. I didn't take any medicine. I didn't listen to the messages on the answering machine. I didn't cry out in my sleep for attention. I didn't light a fire. I didn't talk to the neighbors. I didn't write a book. I didn't suffer humiliation. I didn't notice the difference. I didn't fall headlong from a burning building. I didn't raise and wave my arms in anticipation. I didn't read a newspaper article about people who have stopped traveling to the city. I didn't purchase a compass to shop with. I didn't completely ignore the baby. There, there, Annelisa, don't cry. I didn't record the temperature. I didn't order a new life. I didn't face west when the shadows moved. I didn't have the answer. I didn't move the baby to the other hip. I didn't match the socks. I didn't commit myself to an ideal. I didn't call up my representative. I didn't put out poison for the ants. I didn't remember my dreams. I didn't identify my favorite color. I didn't mistake the green rubber band for a green worm. I didn't discriminate among the faces of adults. I didn't forget the advice of my mother, knowing she exists when not seen. I didn't explore the same activity with each side of my body. I didn't brave one clear moment of desire. I didn't remove the objectionable material. I didn't sense the change of the seasons. I didn't renounce the distance between myself and the world as an illusion. I didn't improve upon the original.

In the Desert a Fool Smiles

In the desert a fool smiles, but doesn't get the joke.

There are only his feet, his plain brown suitcase. The rectangle of light on the wood floor indicating the presence of a door beyond the frame of the picture. It is a soldier's story.

Your sentences are complete. You have not run your sentences together with and.

Do you understand the context. In this sky small and agile motes predominate.

Did the author really see these grains of dark-colored dust.

What he said was it's involuntary. The size of his feet.

Now, for the purposes of planning, you should think of an incident. Forget, however, that it happened to you.

Long speeches are unnatural. As is life itself. The coat and fingers of the gunman, crouching.

It winds up the plot.

Do not attempt to write a story at this time; just a straight description of what happened.

He had the same "good feeling" on the day of the carnival. There remained in the barrack square the blood of a man calling from the ground.

Locate your source material.

I've been listening all my life, you may say. Nearly everyone can listen more effectively than he does.

To indicate another time: next, not long after, finally.

There is a village on the border of the water. It is built of marble, a landscape of light and mineral, and what is purple and round they call, from a distance, a vegetable.

We are indeed in the era and also in the native land of applied science. All Jim could do was grin.

One wishes to suffer in the face of the polite. The screams of pigs and child prodigies.

Other than this a retarded rhythm, a sudden recovery, an airy surprise of rhythm. A procession of desires to change the light.

It erases everything.

The Truth

The truth never arrives in flaming red streams
like the ends of God's hair.
It is the poor gritty dust that comes
from a little box of ammunition,
crusting in the season of rain.
The truth is sediment, rust,
not the shifting logs of dialectics.
It is the end of reason, of all endurance
when one no longer struggles against limitations.
It's funny the way scholars know how everything moves:
how first one thing happens, then another,
how water breaks up into all its parts.
Across the waves we hail one another, the inept
who cannot sail. Perhaps if the stars were clearer,
if there weren't any blackbirds,
if the stars were anchors, pegs.
But then the wind would not blow so far.

Opening Session at the Poetry Conference

1

Only when someone looks at us are we forced to declare ourselves in one or the other state—alive or dead or just arriving from Missouri. The problem is our inability to know. One can get around the dead or alive paradox, of course, with the *many worlds interpretation*. According to that view, there are several parallel universes, some with us dead, others with us alive.

2

We are all without radii or spatial dimension. Pointlike we take shape in the fog like islands or mountains. Unseen dimensions of the universe rolled up within the ones we see. Our existence is a matter of faith in the observer, without whom the world beyond the conference-room windows, the dry coastal hills, even the apparently real storm-dusted ridge of the Sierra Nevada, would be an unclut-tered void.

3

There is a chance, however small, that we might actually be seated on the other side of the room. That we might tunnel through the bridge rather than crossing over it as we had expected. That we might discover, rolled up in the unseen dimensions of ourselves, the initial conditions of the material universe: the leaves on the trees that disappeared last December, impulses from space, the rain out-side sifting steadily down out of a 38 degree fog, or the air inside motionless, uninhabited.

4

No, this is not working. No common ground. Grounding. Separat-ing into discrete entities, not fields but particles, personalities exposing. We have these. Lyric selves. This claiming. This impulse to locate the exact point at which everything falls apart. We are all in this more or less continual state of disarrangement. We are all more or less holding onto the world as it whirls along the corkscrew of time we call our universe. That is why we celebrate, why it is necessary to. Yes, we are all capable of writing poems that fail us.

5

I drive home out of the heat because to return to the fog, to make the transference from the unknown to the known is possible. There are friends I have failed. Perhaps it is because they have unlisted numbers. I call my mother to reassure her that she is alive. Her mother, her Aunt Eda, her father, even my father, all of them, she reminds me, died on a Sunday. Or close to Sunday. This being Tuesday, we appear to be safe.

This is not working, I tell her. There is still the fog which, although good for the leaves, is growing thicker. And then there are always the dead to be removed from the lawn.

Nobody ever calls, she complains to me. *Not even my children.*

6

It is this way with words. Sounds of islands, the Bahamas. Sonnets composed by the dead. Theology, history, the occult. The act of looking at them turns them into particles we can identify. They appear in a room at the end of the hall. Like gifts. Like cradle sounds. Parodies of ourselves.

At the End of the Season the Apples

At the end of the season the apples droop over the lobelia.
They make room for themselves in my flower boxes.
It's O.K. with me. The time for pruning and sweeping the yard
clear of debris is coming. Waiting patiently allows
the disorder of my life a kind of grace, the natural desire of all things.
Sometimes late at night I fall asleep on the couch deliberately,
avoiding the rituals of going to bed: brushing my teeth,
buttoning my nightgown, clearing the air of arguments
to make room for two separate lives in the same room,
to make peace with the darkness we are about to
trust ourselves to. This is all so much work, and it is late,
and the sleep I allow to rush over me, completely unprepared,
is rich and dream-laden and satisfying, as if I had come back
to my native language.

NARRATIONS LEADING TO THE NUMBER NINE

Narrations Leading to the Number Nine

Coming to the edge of ourselves, living at the edges.
By these we are connected. We hover, so to speak, in the air.

"I haven't got it," she said. "Here I am an aboriginal person,
and I've lost my Dreaming."

She had only fragments.

In 1969 a man in a house by the sea, in a small seacoast town, turns
over the ninth Tarot card. Meaning the story line, the plot, the
vector of my life. Another man, dressed in a gray robe, holds out a
lantern to light the way in the dark up a steep mountain slope.
Having lived a long time, he has already reached the summit. He
arrived in another age. Or he has always arrived. I take this to mean
something and begin braiding my hair. I am looking for a pattern, a
connection which must be made. I am required to make it: the
fringe of yarn at the edge of the blanket, strips of leather, cattail
stems. The loose ends fly out behind me in the tidal world. I am
riding a dark stallion bareback up the slope of the hill above the
seacoast town. I have lost hold of the reins and must cling with my
knees, twist my fingers in the thick hair of his black mane. I sail out
of myself, far out on a little boat of fear. In the night the horse leaps
out of himself too, clatters through the empty streets. He knows the
passage out and moves that way.

You come to the edge of yourself,
ungathered,
full of desire,

as in the night when you want so much,
as in childhood when you are forgiven.

By this are we connected,
this space between us, this sense of non-being.

When I looked into the winter above me
too many souls, worlds beyond worlds,
I did not know which one I walked in.

In 1969 in a small seacoast town in the winter of my thirteenth year,
I walked to the edge of the Greenwood Pier. This was the end of my
element. I had discovered no other. The wind blew a fine spray up
from the heaving surface onto the splinters of collapsed beams. If I
were to fall asleep out here, I might roll off into the green waters
below. I would not be coming back. Too much had already been
abandoned.

The stars above seemed but a boneyard in the sky,
circling dithyrambically
in the shapes of human beasts.

Men and the powers colliding.

True, you did not desire this world
nor your particular existence in it.

You dream stem-legs, graceful
reed-fronds
a wind blows through you
the quick core of you quivers, sings
a small note
deep in the throat

I had come to the edge, breathing hard, studying the line that divided me from the seacoast town. How long, I wondered, would such a line continue? Was I expected to climb the mountain, follow the figure in gray with the lantern? A self—not mine, but another's—was already moving ahead of me, pacing the steep slope, hoping to arrive before night fell. She thought perhaps I had fallen asleep and rolled off the abandoned ruins of the pier into the tide. From her height it was clearer what had come before and after. But here, in this small seacoast town, in the winter of my thirteenth year, I could not find the connection. Loose ends fraying, splitting away. If I walked in my body I did not recognize myself as a woman ascending the mountain trail in the dusk.

in the wilderness
the thing you longed for or dreaded,
the thing that lives in your mind
and cannot be exorcised

a dream

an absolute key

The horse was old and skittish, as if he had caught the scent of death descending from the wooded mountain above the seacoast town. He lifted his head, curling up his lips, revealing huge teeth striated brown and white, and pink, fleshy gums. This was an animal, no dream, no story. Although most of my life seemed invented in the winter of that year, this was real, his horse-teeth, his black eyes, his nostrils fierce and searching. He curled his lips and let out a scream, leaping over the fence and down to the edge of the water where in the dark his iron shoes and hooves kicked up from the wet sand a blue fluorescence.

PAPYRUS:

A TEMPORARY

JOURNEY

The following poem sequence is based on
PAPYRUS HARRIS 500:
Song Cycle III

Papyrus

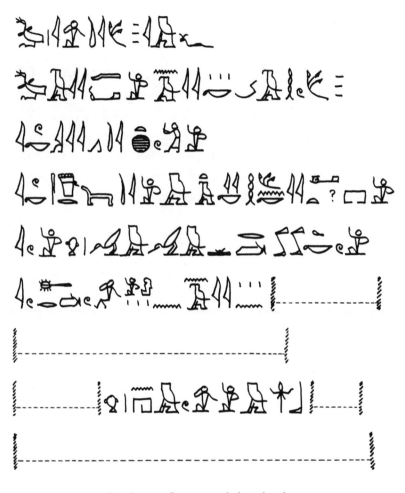

> *I strip you of your tangled garlands,*
>
> Once you are back again, O drunken man
>
> > *sprawled deep in sleep (and gone) in bed.*
>
> I stroke your feet
>
> > *while children . . .*
>
> > > *[Here the papyrus begins to tatter.]*
>
> *. . . cry out wild with longing . . .*
>
> > *[The rest is lost.]*

Translated by John L. Foster

A man floats in the air over the rising moon. We understand so little. He is sleeping in the air, his head resting easily on the question. The moon opens like an eye. It sees the question but not the man. The eye is empty, the man was made without arms of any kind, without legs, only a penis resting, like the body it belongs to, inside a box. In the light from the moon the man might be taken for a clock. She has made many mistakes. One was seeing the key as a man.

These legs are running. He says, *I stroke your feet,* as if he understood what a woman feels in the presence of a drunken man. As if a woman could still feel longing, could cry out wildly *while children . . . or a drunken man . . . sprawled deep in sleep.* There are dreams you run up your legs like flags when the wind is kicking. But are they dreams or repetitions of the past? It is only this: a pair of legs running, a pair of notes whistling in the dark.

This is the way I make my point BANG
This is the way I make you see BANG
Break your bones BANG
Break your BANG dust
BANG your head BANG

A lake. A night without a moon. Distant memory of what the sun looks like rising. The darkness blows across the water like a wind. Passions that cool with age.

The eye begins to open. A woman's pleasure opening. A man wears a hat and salutes. He is the inspector general. She has just a small part in this.

Further down

while the man sleeps he holds his weapon. It looks like a sun, a comet with a long tail. Death and the hours of devotion. The door to her pleasure lies open. He cannot reach her. Her pleasure, her lips, float in a world beyond him.

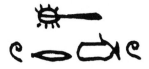

Where is the woman now? Where is her body? A comet blazes in the air above her, dragging the dark lake in its tail. This may be what the sun looks like, rising. She doesn't see it this way. She doesn't see he has laid down his weapon and gone to sleep. She has asked him to turn away. Now they are both without power. They play the scene again and again till all pleasure is gone, diminishing to a harmless comma, a life empty of ambition. Small snakes.

Here is a ridiculous bird. She cries out long into the
night, falling through her days, her ordinary life.

memories:
a coffin; some aspect of the dream
that is being confined.

She remembers a song from her youth, a
melody, a line around the empty space.

This emptiness is a dead thing, a wild beast
stung with spears. Outside are many terrible
sounds knocking a hole in the coffin wall. A
door to the inside.

She does not know it is her occupation to walk the boundary between the dead and the silence of her ordinary life. She understands so little. She kneels beside a coffin, singing. She has tied herself to the mast so as not to drown. The white lines rise and swell across the landscape. But how to become the hero of the story, the one who rises, bright and visible, out of stone?

He curls up under the weight of his anger. Puts his hands deeper into his pockets so he no longer has to touch anyone. When he wakes up in the morning it pushes him out of bed downstairs to make coffee. When he falls asleep in the sun it runs deep below him like the water table. In the early evening it comes on like a sore headache, tension along the length of the back. He confuses this with the need for coffee or sleep or exercise.

She says, "I know the goodness of my land,
    whiskery ears,
   insignificant birds,
    sickle-shaped
     silver, blue."

He says, "what is this fatal
    outburst of emotion?"

ʃ   A snake is easier to recognize.

The final fork of lightning. Half a cradle, a scythe, something to dismantle the hours. Between the drums and the animals. She dare not leave it exposed, so she tucks it inside her where it will send tiny murderous messages years after the papers have been filed.

Sometimes their legs appear in the water. They go on walking like shorebirds in the wind. How is it they do not see the water disappearing?

How is it these legs stride forward, clear of purpose, without the half of themselves they have lost?

There are waterfalls in the rainforest tangled up in this life. Her hair tumbles down her back in a long braid. It buys expensive rooms high above the city. Boats fall out of the horizon into the ocean, traveling long white wakes as they come back to the bay. She is made of two strands. Now she braids her long hair with flowers.

Ribbon blades
bright
sharp
piercing

What she winds around her neck is lovely like a storm over a sum-
mer garden. Her limbs sway in the night. Not yet asleep, he says,
I strip you of your tangled garlands, knowing something dangerous is
left behind when the storm passes.

Her beads will break,

~~~~~~ clattering over the floor

She cries out long into the night. It is a wild night, storms moving south, shaking the dead beast he keeps inside. She lies on her back in the dark tracing a line around her. A box of light in the darkness.

When you are driving like this in a storm, you know you might kill something. Or if it is still alive, it might move in and press against you, sleeping.

In the morning she stoops to gather them up, each red drop.

The ghost of a child appears in the unoccupied air above the morn-
ing. They sail small smiles like boats to and fro across the breakfast
table. Before the days of easy conversation, before the teacup, before
the documents, a stone hollowed in the middle, a single drop of oil.
Visiting spirits. Naked food. Placed inside her, this may keep her
from falling into his plans. She'll scoop a fish out of the air.

Terry Ehret was born in San Francisco and grew up in the Bay Area. She received her B.A. in psychology from Stanford University in 1977, and an M.A. in Creative Writing from San Francisco State University in 1984. She teaches English at Santa Rosa Junior College and lives with her husband and three daughters in Petaluma, California.

This cold river flows between them at night, asleep in their separate lives like parallel worlds. It is a dark barge, a long river, a temporary journey.